The Pocket Book of Good Grannies

Jane Fearnley-Whittingstall
with illustrations by Alex Fox

Published in 2011 by Short Books
Short Books
3A Exmouth House
Pine Street
EC1R 0JH

10 9 8 7 6 5 4 3 2 1

A CIP catalogue record for this book
is available from the British Library.

ISBN 978-1-907595-50-9
Printed in Great Britain by Clays, Suffolk

Contents

When I am an old woman, I shall wear purple
with a red hat that doesn't go...

Jenny Joseph

Introduction

Grannies come in all shapes and sizes, and in a rich diversity of temperaments, talents and lifestyles. But they all have one thing in common, the special relationship that is such a wonderful compensation for getting older – the bond between grandparent and grandchild.

No wonder that grannies, when they get together – and however different they are – always have plenty to talk about. Such conversations, along with memories of my own grandparents and my mother and mother-in-law, have been the inspiration for this collection of affectionate portraits. Here are grannies ancient and modern, town and country, glamorous and cosy.

I hope readers will recognise the grandmothers in their lives, or perhaps in themselves. Most of us are composites. One of my grandmothers was definitely DiY Granny and I see traces of her in me. I also try to be Hands-on Granny and Cuddly Granny too – though I don't always succeed.

I am hugely grateful to Alex Fox for his brilliant granny drawings. He has captured us all!

Jane Fearnley-Whittingstall,
October 2011

Action Gran

Abseiling, scuba diving, trekking in the Himalayas –
you name it, Action Gran is up for it.

Busy though she is, she still finds time at week-
ends to get a picnic together and take the grandchildren on a bear hunt or a hike to the local beauty
spot, so their parents can enjoy a day on their own.
Her get-up-and-go attitude is equally useful on
holiday – she is the one who organises beach cricket
and can be seen out at sea in her wetsuit, waiting
with the children and their surfboards for the biggest
wave.

I have had a go at being Action Gran, earning a
modest reputation as maker of the best-ever bows
and arrows. But to my shame I failed the maggot test.
This involves spiking the aforesaid wriggling live bait
with a fishing hook. Denise, my co-granny, does
it without turning a hair.

Army Granny

This granny grew up in an army family, always on the move from one rented house to another, and always changing schools. Her own grandmother was the one fixed star in her childhood firmament and she is determined to be the same.

Army Granny knows that every battle ground needs a good general, and in the family she is indisputably in command. She threatens mutinous troops with loss of privileges or confinement to barracks, and is always good for her word. Her grandchildren learn from an early age that brave soldiers never cry when they fall off their bikes, and never say, 'it wasn't my fault.' Her bark is far worse than her bite – she adores her grandchildren and will do anything for them.

Arty Granny

Arty Granny has always felt she was an *artiste manquée*. Now at last she has time to pursue her true calling. She has an easel in the conservatory and daubs happily away all day long, blissfully unaware of the passage of time. She knows her pictures aren't great art but she doesn't care. She wears her paint-stained smock with pride, and wraps her hair in a Bohemian scarf. Her studio is everything a grandchild could dream of.

Arty Granny's role model is Grandma Moses, whose paintings hang in nine museums in the United States and in Vienna and Paris. She painted her first picture at the age of 76 when arthritis in her hands forced her to give up embroidery. It was the first of more than 1,000 pictures, twenty-five of them done after she had passed her 100th birthday.

Competitive Granny

Competitive Granny would never dream of letting the youngest grandchild win at *Snakes and Ladders*. What would be the point? If you play, you play to win.

She's so keen to beat all comers at everything that she was once seen giving her croquet ball a tiny nudge with her toe, to move it closer to the hoop. There were triumphant shrieks, 'Granny, you *cheated!* We *saw* you.'

Competitive Granny has no truck with such accusations. Whether it's Grandmother's Footsteps or three sets of tennis, you can count on her to keep the children busy for hours on end. Her mantra: 'Don't be a bad loser, darling.'

Cuddly Granny

My own mummy was anything but yummy. Her build was ample; she applied make-up twice a year and always wore sensible shoes, that is, if she remembered to change out of her slippers before fetching us from school. Her grandchildren loved her dearly.

Contrary to popular belief, this type of granny is not extinct. She's alive and well – her cottage-loaf figure, her grey hair and specs, cardigan and handbag full of sweeties, can be found in a park near you. While her grandchildren are hurtling around the playground, she remains always a picture of benevolent calm.

When Cuddly Granny gets them home she will fill them up with cake and cocoa before settling down on the sofa for a story. Her head is a vast repository of nursery rhymes, songs and lullabies and she knows many traditional fairy tales by heart. But her grandchildren's favourite are the ones she makes up as she goes along. They often start 'Once upon a time there was a very naughty boy called...'

Culture Vulture Granny

Culture Vulture Granny thinks her grandchildren are complete philistines. 'How can you read/watch/listen to that rubbish?' she cries. To convert them, she takes them to operas, ballets and Shakespeare plays; to the National Gallery, the Tate and the V&A.

Truth be told, the children are dragged rather reluctantly to these treats, but Culture Vulture Granny has a gift for communicating her own enthusiasm. She also knows that half an hour of art is worth an ice cream, and an hour is worth a pizza. So her phrase 'You'll enjoy it when you get there' usually turns out to be true.

DiY Gran

Every time you go to DiY Gran's house something has changed. Because whenever she's feeling restless DiY granny re-tiles the bathroom or paints the kitchen – again.

She loves a challenge and when something needs doing, she gets on and does it, wielding any tool that comes to hand, from the Black & Decker to the corkscrew, though she may not always put them to the use they were designed for. The dirtier the job, the happier DiY Gran is. She thinks nothing of sticking her arm down a drain to remove a blockage.

My paternal grandmother was a DiY Gran before DiY was invented. She stood on tables to change light bulbs, shifted wardrobes single-handed and changed the oil in the car. Patience was not one of her virtues. If my grandfather tried to help, she would give him short shrift.

DiY Gran can be a wonderful asset to her family. She finds it hard to sit still, so when she comes to stay, it's a good idea to have a project for her to get stuck into. Perhaps there's a new carpet to be laid, or the garage needs clearing out. Her grandchildren look forward to her Christmas and birthday presents, which tend to be practical: one year an electric screwdriver, the next a classic multi-bladed penknife complete with gadget for getting stones out of horses' hooves.

DJ Granny

Ruth Flowers started a dazzling new career as a disc jockey after discovering dance music at her grandson's birthday party. 'It was very noisy and the lights were flashing,' she told a reporter, 'but there was an awful lot of energy and joy.'

She learned her trade from a French producer and now plays 'a mix of old-school hits, electrobeat and bling-bling style' (don't ask) at fashionable venues in Paris and the South of France. She wears a green satin bomber jacket, eye-catching earrings and huge dark glasses, with her white hair brushed up into a punk-ish halo. 'It's a little glammy,' Ruth says, 'a bit over the top, but it fits the bill. I mean, if I appeared in a cardigan and brogue shoes it wouldn't be quite the same.'

DJ Granny, though not exactly a common type, has much to teach us, both about having fun and taking up new opportunities – whatever age we may be...

Doggy Granny

When you go into Doggy Granny's flat or get into her car you will be overwhelmed by the smell of dog, and either joyous barking or ear-splitting yapping. If Granny trains her dogs strictly, the noise will be accompanied with a frenzied wagging of tails. If she's been indulgent with them, they will jump up and lick your face – and knock you over if you are a nervous toddler.

My doggy grandmother often gave us jobs to do. Most were quite pleasurable but when the metal comb and canister of DDT powder appeared, we tended mysteriously to disappear. None of us wanted to de-flea Tufton, her bad-tempered Pekinese.

For dog-loving children, a visit to Doggy Granny can be pure pleasure. Neither child nor dog ever seems to tire of the game where child throws ball, dog fetches it, dog refuses to give it to child, child bawls, and granny takes the ball back from dog ready to start the whole thing again... And, best of all, there may even be a new puppy to play with.

Doggy Granny loves her dogs as much as she loves her grandchildren, and she sometimes gets them confused, reciting the names of half a dozen dogs and children before she arrives at the correct one. She is a fund of funny dog stories, which her grandchildren beg her to relate again and again. 'Tell us about the time Rex ate the picnic...'

Dressing-up Granny

My grandmother's dressing-up box came out only on special occasions – on the third day of non-stop rain, perhaps, or at Christmas when the grandchildren decided to put on a show for the grown-ups.

Out of the trunk would emerge sequined jackets, slippers with heels like cotton-reels, a yellow satin clown suit with huge silk pompoms, artificial flowers and an orange-blossom bridal wreath. There were fragments of army and naval uniforms, wooden swords, a child's sailor suit and a collapsible opera hat.

As soon as Dressing-up Granny gave the word, we children would scramble to grab the best things, only for her to beat us to it. She did more than join in the fun – draped in beads, scarves and cloaks in rainbow colours, she would elbow us out of way, parading and posturing in front of the full-length mirror, and keeping up a running commentary on ball gowns, cocktail frocks and the Ascot hats of her youth.

Gambling Granny

I've just got here, through Paris, from the sunny
                                        southern shore;
I to Monte Carlo went, just to raise my winter's rent.
Dame Fortune smiled upon me as she'd never done
                                        before,
And I've now such lots of money, I'm a gent.
Yes, I've now such lots of money, I'm a gent.

As I walk along the Bois Boolong
With an independent air
You can hear the girls declare
'He must be a Millionaire.'
You can hear them sigh and wish to die,
You can see them wink the other eye
At the man who broke the bank at Monte Carlo.

'The Man Who Broke the Bank at Monte Carlo' –
a Music Hall song composed by Fred Gilbert in 1892.

She may not be the gran who broke the bank at
Monte Carlo, but she regales her grandchildren with
stories of glamorous casinos in days gone by, not
only dear old Monte Carlo but Le Touquet, just a
hop across the Channel. Gambling is in this granny's

blood, and she can't resist passing on her passion to a new generation. She prepares the children for a misspent youth by getting them to play *vingt-et-un* with real money. She has an account with a bookmaker, and most afternoons the grandchildren have to keep quiet while she watches racing on Channel 4.

Depending on the parents' attitude, Gambling Granny is either an Awful Warning for the children, or Leading Them Astray. But she is definitely giving them a good grounding in maths.

Glam Gran

She descends on the newborn's cradle like a fairy
godmother, bearing gifts of designer baby clothes,
cashmere wraps and Tiffany teething rings. In the
bad old days before disposable nappies, one such
granny arrived in the maternity ward with a present
for her daughter-in-law, a friend of mine.
It was an exquisite satin and lace nightgown and
negligée. But all Jenny could see as she gazed at
this generous present were the £-signs adding up to
rather more than the price of a longed-for washing
machine.

Glam Gran will never be the nappy-changing,
nose-wiping type. She may take the baby in her
arms for a cuddle, but as soon as she detects damp at
either end, she passes the parcel. She doesn't really do
babies, darling. But she will come into her own when
her grandchildren are older, helping them paint their
toenails, giving them brilliant presents and thinking
up wonderful treats.

Glasto Granny

Aka Boho Granny and Hippy Granny. In her heyday she wore flowers in her hair and waded through the Glastonbury mud to scream ecstatically at Van Morrison, Ian Drury and Elvis Costello. She's played her favourite songs over and over to her grandchildren, and they now can sing along happily to 'Bridge over Troubled Water', 'Let it Be' and 'Won't get Fooled Again'.

She still owns an embroidered Afghan sheepskin coat and lends it to her teen grandchildren for special occasions. Another treasured relic is her Biba maxi dress, with its psychedelic print. She's on a strict diet, hoping to wear it again when her grandchildren take her to the Big Chill.

Globe-trotting Granny

Globe-trotting Granny has got the travelling bug.
She intends to have been there, done everything
before she dies: Angkor Wat, Machu Picchu, the
Great Barrier Reef, the Taj Mahal – you name it, it's
on her wish list.

This granny is thrilled to be asked to look after
her grandchildren at half term, although make
sure you have a back-up plan, as she will have no
compunction about crying off a few weeks before
when a friend of hers offers her a place on a
trip canoeing down the Amazon.

If she's not around much, though, Globe-trotting
Granny more than compensates when she does pay
a visit, armed with exotic presents and an outlandish
story to tell. 'You see, we were on the trail of a snow
leopard in the Himalayas...'

Google Gran

Grannies over a certain age may find the term IT confusing. They know what 'It' meant in their day. It was the same thing as 'SA', or Sex Appeal. 'Douglas Fairbanks', my great grandmother used to say with a far-away look, 'had oodles of It.'

Google Gran is totally at home with a different sort of IT. She has a Blackberry in her handbag and never travels without her laptop. She has her own blog and keeps in touch weekly with her expat chums by Skype. Ask her where her new antique sideboard came from, and she will tell you she bought it on ebay...

Just beware Google Gran becoming friends on Facebook with her grandchildren – with-it though she is, she might not always like what she sees...

Gourmet Granny

Sartre wrote, '... I could make my grandmother go into raptures of joy just by being hungry,' and this seems to be a general rule for Gourmet Grannies.

My own mother is remembered by her grand-children for, among other things, her Rum Babas. I don't think she would have minded my describing her as a greedy granny (takes one to know one) and, had she not been, she would not have been such a marvellous cook. She loved food and loved cooking, so her kitchen was an exciting place to be. Her own happiness was complete if there was at least one small person with her to roll out a pastry man with currant eyes and buttons, and lick the cake bowl clean.

You'll know Gourmet Granny from the delicious smells wafting out of her kitchen, and the light dusting of flour on the tip of her nose...

Granny in Denial

'There's no way I'm going to be known as 'Granny' or 'Grandma', says this glamorous blonde grandmother-in-waiting. She won't be written off as a member of the grey-hair-and-baggy-cardigan brigade, and who can blame her? Secretly she wants to be mistaken for the au pair. She encourages her grandchildren to call her by her first name, or a variation on it.

Granny in Denial is definitely not ready to take on full grandmotherly responsibilities. It seems only yesterday that her student children were bringing their laundry home and raiding the larder. Now all of a sudden they're breeding, and expecting her to look after them all over again... No, thanks. This granny's got plenty more living to do!

Granny Down-Under
(Antipodean Granny)

If you dig a deep enough hole you get to Australia. There you will find Granny Down-Under, upside-down and waltzing with a kangaroo. Sadly, owing to distance and expensive air fares, she only sees her grandchildren once every three years, but they think of her every bedtime when they snuggle up with their furry koala bears and she doesn't seem so far away. They like to sing her songs and repeat her jokes, such as:

Q: 'What's a bison?'
A: 'It's what an Austrilian washes his fice in.'

Once a jolly swagman camped by a billabong
Under the shade of a coolibah tree,
And he sang as he watched and waited till his billy boiled
'You'll come a-waltzing Matilda, with me
Waltzing Matilda, waltzing Matilda
You'll come a-waltzing Matilda, with me'
And he sang as he watched and waited till his billy boiled,
'You'll come a-waltzing Matilda, with me'.

Down came a jumbuck to drink at that billabong,

Up jumped the swagman and grabbed him with glee,
And he sang as he shoved that jumbuck in his tucker bag,
'You'll come a-waltzing Matilda, with me'.

Granny Greenfingers

She lives, eats and sleeps gardening and longs to share her passion with a new generation. When her first grandchild, plonked down on the lawn, reaches out to grab a daisy, she thinks 'Green genes'. She holds buttercups under toddlers' chins to see if they like butter, tells the time for them with dandelion clocks, makes ballerinas from poppies and shows them how to sip nectar from a honeysuckle. She has the grandchildren lisping '*Escholtzia californica*' and '*Nasticreechia Krorluppia*' before they can say their own names.

She makes gardening fun, giving rides in the wheelbarrow and organising competitions for who can find the biggest leaf, the smallest flower, or the most snails. From an early age each child has his own plot in Granny's garden. Not the no-go area by the rubbish heap, but a sunny spot with good soil, and she takes the children shopping for radish, lettuce and sunflower seeds to sow there. Between visits she weeds their patch so they won't get discouraged, and when their crops are ready to harvest, they celebrate together.

Granny from Hell

One version of this alarming species of granny was the character immortalised in the 1950s and 60s by the cartoonist Giles. He showed grandma riding a motorbike, at the head of a posse of Hell's Angels, terrorising the neighbourhood.

In fact, the Granny from Hell has been around for centuries – think of the witch in *Hansel and Gretel*, or terrifying, iron-toothed Baba Yaga, the Russian demon who lived in a house on chicken's legs (rather like her own, presumably...) And let's not forget the granny in our own well-loved fairy tale, *Little Red Riding Hood*, who metamorphoses from a gentle, harmless old lady into a wicked wolf.

The Granny from Hell still exists today, of course – rude, inappropriately dressed and enormous fun. Just don't expect her to help with the homework.

Granny Upstairs

Even today, lots of families house their Aged Ps on the premises. The granny flat may be in the attic, over the garage, or in the basement. Having granny (and/or grandpa) on the spot means there's a built-in babysitter and always someone at home to welcome latch-key kids with tea, sympathy and a bottomless biscuit tin. It also saves parents those twice-yearly, cross-country visits to the old folk, with two car-sick children in the back and strong feelings of guilt for not having visited for six months.

But don't take Granny Upstairs too much for granted. While she's glad of the company of her grandchildren (most of the time), she's also secretly rather enjoying her new-found freedom. No longer burdened by the responsibilities of running her own house, she has a flourishing new social life. Her only concern is that she might wake the grandchildren when she creeps back in after a night on the tiles.

Greenham Granny

This granny is proud of her radical credentials.
As a teenager she joined the Campaign for Nuclear
Disarmament and once marched to Aldermaston
(well, some of the way) chanting 'Ban the Bomb.'
Twenty years later she joined the Greenham
Common Women's Peace Camp.

Her children grew up rather embarrassed by
their mother's political extremism. Their own views
are middle-of-the-road and they describe hers as
'tiresome'.

Nowadays she is always on about global
warming. Her grandchildren listen even if their
parents don't. The eldest stood as a candidate for the
Green Party in his school's mock General Election,
Granny lent him a soap box and even helped him
write his speech.

Hands-on Granny

Hands-on Granny knows by instinct how to get a burp out of a baby and comfort a colicky one. She doesn't notice the smell of baby vomit and won't mind if her grandchild messes up her hair and sticks his fingers up her nose. Instead of Glam Gran's gift of a cashmere wrap, her offering to the newborn is a hand-knitted matinée jacket with matching bootees and bonnet. She always has tissues about her person for mopping up dribble and wiping noses, and will spend hours on the floor playing with toddlers. Nothing is too much trouble for Hands-on Granny who will come to the rescue at a moment's notice. Both her daughter and her daughter-in-law ask for her advice and even act on it, because she really does know all about babies and gives her advice tactfully.

In fact she's nearly perfect – so she's probably not you, and she's certainly not me!

Health and Safety Gran

Parents can have total confidence in leaving the kids with Health and Safety Gran.

In her house there are child-proof catches on all the windows, and she's had the locks on the loo door raised up out of a toddler's reach. As soon as her first grandchild shows signs of learning to walk, she installs a stair gate.

Meanwhile, the kitchen worktops and floor, the bath and basin are all washed daily with a product that kills 99% of household germs. It's the other 1% she's worried about, so when in charge she takes care that the baby, too, gets a thorough daily wash, paying attention to every nook and cranny. After a few days with Health and Safety Gran, he is the cleanest baby in the world – though his babygro is bursting its poppers because she has boil-washed all his clothes.

High-maintenance Granny

'I don't want to be a nuisance in the morning, darling, so why don't I just have breakfast on a tray in my room? A cup of Earl Grey, really weak. And some toast would be lovely, granary if you've got it. And perhaps a boiled egg...'

It's true that taking High-maintenance Granny breakfast in bed is less trouble than having her hovering in the kitchen asking with one breath what she can do to help and, with the next, how to fill the kettle. And she's fine for the rest of the day, just as long as she can occupy the only bathroom for an hour after breakfast, and have her Dubonnet and soda at exactly 6.45 pm.

Truth be told, her grandchildren rather enjoy waiting on this granny. They search out a rarely-used cup and saucer instead of a mug and make posies for her breakfast tray. It's good practice for Mother's Day – and there's usually a little reward for their efforts... High-maintenance Granny is no fool!

In-my-day Granny

In her day, she and her siblings were allowed *either* butter or jam on their bread, never both. She had to walk two miles to school and two miles back. Children had to be in bed with lights out at 6.30pm. Sweets were rationed and she didn't see a banana until she was six years old.

On the other hand... in her day they made daisy chains and found four-leaf clovers; the postman came twice a day; they made fudge on rainy afternoons; trains had restaurant cars where you were served tea and toasted tea-cakes and there were Punch and Judy shows on the beach.

If sometimes this granny seems to rabbit on a bit, just remember: her astonishingly good memory will come in extremely useful for her grandchildren's history projects. There's nothing she can't tell you about life during and after World War II.

Know-it-all Granny

Some grannies (and granddads) are only happy when they are in charge. In the car they prefer to be at the wheel, but will drive from the back seat if they have to. Whether it's a question of which TV channel to watch, or what to put on the shopping list, *they* must make the decisions.

At big family occasions such as Christmas or Easter, Know-it-all Granny is in her element, masterminding the menus, present lists and decorations. As for childcare, she is supremely confident – she knows how to get a baby to sleep through the night, how often to feed it, and when to wean it. It's no use quoting the advice of modern child-care gurus to Know-it-all Granny. She'll never admit there could be a better method than hers. And, strangely enough, she's often right.

Mad Granny

In a parent, eccentricity is not usually considered
a desirable quality, but in a grandparent it is more
than acceptable. I recently saw a seven-year-old boy
announce to a television interviewer, 'My granddad is
absolutely bonkers', and it was said with real pride.

'Bonkers' would also have been an apt descrip-
tion of Diana Holman-Hunt's paternal grandmother, described in Diana's funny and touching
book, *My Grandmothers and I*. The widow of the
pre-Raphaelite painter Holman Hunt, she lived in
solitary squalor in a large, cold house near Holland
Park, stuffed full of pictures, furniture and *objets*,
from Italian Renaissance Old Master paintings to a
thunderbolt found on the South Downs by Edward
Lear and a bundle of Lord Kitchener's letters. She set
up burglar alarms each night, home-made from bells
on tripwires and piles of tins, and often fell over them
herself, creating a fearful din.

Make Do and Mend Granny

This granny will have a button box and a scrap bag. 'A stitch in time saves nine', she says as she rummages for the right needle for the job, and the right shade of denim for a patch.

The announcement of a pregnancy sends her straight to the wool shop for knitting needles and a few balls of 3-ply. The hat she knits when baby is born may disappear without trace after its first tactful appearance but the jumper and trousers she makes for Teddy will be cherished for many years. She cuts up old sheets for use as dusters, and for years she's been hoarding Grandpa's old boxer shorts, ready to make bunting for her granddaughter's wedding.

Man Gran

No, this is not a granny with a moustache and a habit of sitting with her legs wide apart. It's a grandpa who happens to like babies, and looks after his grandchildren hands on. Today's fathers don't think twice about bathing babies and changing nappies, but it's rare to find a grandfather prepared to go through the messy routine.

As soon as the parents' maternity leave comes to an end, Man Gran volunteers for childcare duties three days a week, and is blissfully happy bonding with his grandson. Granny is happy, too – it means her afternoon Bridge games aren't disrupted, and that her recently-retired husband isn't at a loose end.

Old-fashioned Granny

Old-fashioned Granny would never dream of dying her grey hair. She keeps her good navy skirt for best and wears slippers in the house to save the highly-polished shoes she has had for decades.

This granny is probably shocked by the way her daughter or daughter-in-law brings up her babies, but she will be philosophical about it and accept that things have changed. The one thing she cannot abide is bad manners. But don't for a minute think Old-fashioned Granny is boring. In her house, she has a gramophone with a collection of Flapper music on old 78's. She loves nothing more than to teach her grandchildren how to dance the Charleston.

Proverbial Granny

A swarm of bees in May is worth a load of hay;
a swarm of bees in June is worth a silver spoon;
but a swarm in July isn't worth a fly

If a grandchild asks Proverbial Granny an awkward question, she's unlikely to get a straight answer. 'Curiosity killed the cat,' 'Ask no questions and you'll be told no lies' and 'Ask a silly question and you'll get a silly answer' are typical responses. The reply to 'how old are you, Granny?' is 'As old as my tongue and a little older than my teeth.'

For just about every situation, there's a saying, a motto or an old wives' tale, and Granny knows them all. 'A little dirt never hurt anyone,' she says, when baby rubs mud into her hair. 'There'll be tears before bedtime' when the children get over-excited. In the kitchen, a watched pot never boils and it's no use crying over spilt milk, but many hands make light work and a little of what you fancy does you good.

At bath-time cleanliness is next to godliness, obviously. And early to bed and early to rise makes a man healthy, wealthy and wise.

In the wider world, a fool and his money are soon

parted, a friend in need is a friend indeed, and all's well that ends well. As for teaching your grandmother to suck eggs....

Rock 'n' Roll Gran

She may or may not have qualified for her bus pass
but it is completely irrelevant, since she makes no
concessions to her age or her granny status either in
the way she dresses or with her lifestyle in general.
Daughters and daughters-in-law often despair of
Rock'n'roll Gran, complaining about 'the
smoking and drinking, the junk food and the late
nights', but they forgive everything because granny
and her grandchildren are madly in love with each
other.

Often a self-confessed bad mother, she makes
up for it with the new generation, providing
endless fun, and turning out to be a fund of worldly-
wise advice.

Royal Granny

Queen Victoria (24 May 1819 – 22 January 1901), was sometimes known as the 'Grandmother of Europe'. And not surprisingly, seeing that, of her 42 grandchildren, 26 married into European royal and noble families. Two became kings: Kaiser Wilhelm of Germany and King George V of England. And seven of Queen Victoria's granddaughters married kings (Greece, Finland, Norway, Sweden, Russia, Romania, Spain).

When Victoria's first grandchild was born she wrote to her daughter, 'A grandmother must ever be loved and venerated, particularly one's mother's mother, I always think.'

You might be forgiven for thinking that the words 'We are a Grandmother' were spoken by a Royal Granny. No. They were Prime Minister Margaret Thatcher's way of announcing the birth of her first grandchild.

Sporty Granny

She breezes in, straight off the golf course or the tennis court, radiating energy. Following the principle that the children will have fun if granny is having fun, and granny will have fun if she is doing what she enjoys, Sporty Grannies can be counted on to share their enthusiasm with their grandchildren and get them off to a good start in their chosen sports.

She'll happily turn out to watch a grandchild playing rugby for the third eleven, running up and down on the side lines, shouting 'Support, support' and 'Tackle.' When it comes to football she can even explain the offside rule. And during the cricket season, it's off to the park where Sporty Granny is equally happy batting, bowling or fielding.

Student Gran

When Student Gran left school at 16, her ambition was to get married and live happily ever after. In her day most women didn't go to university and they had jobs, not careers. But, boy, is she making up for lost time. She already has an Open University degree in Philosophy and Psychology, and now she's signed up to learn Russian at the local college so she can read *Anna Karenina* as Tolstoy wrote it.

This granny has taken to student life like a duck to water. She wears jeans and a Che Guevara T-shirt (there's a blast from the past) and hangs out at the 'in' café with her fellow-students, some of whom are her grandchildren's age. She has even smoked a joint behind the college bike shed – *and* inhaled.

'The Bolter' aka Sugar Granny

This granny is past 70 – and still getting divorced and remarried. Her latest husband is younger than her youngest son, more toy-boy than husband, and she showers him with presents.

The Bolter's children have lost count of her husbands – they only know she's serious competition for Joan Collins. And they have long since stopped turning up to her wedding celebrations. (There are only so many times you can attend a reception on a tropical beach...)

Her grandchildren, however, know the names of all their long lost grandpas. They're the ones who still come up trumps every Christmas.

Supergran

It's you, of course. And me. We probably all aspire to be Supergran – and, oddly enough, many of us get pretty close. The truth is that, because of the phenomenon of mutual, unconditional love, our grandchildren in their naive and trusting way often believe us to be utterly unbeatable in every way. We may feel inadequate compared to those perfect grannies who devote all their time and energy to their relationship with their grandchildren, but we give what we are able to. And anyway it can be a mistake to be over-zealous.

The ideal grandmother, according to one happy daughter-in-law I know, 'never gives advice unless directly asked, never criticises my methods of child-rearing, just plays with the children, listens to them and talks to them'. It's quality, not quantity, of attention that's most important.

Wise Granny

Wise Granny plays a vitally important role in this modern digital age, keeping the traditional culture alive. She is also custodian of her family's history. How would I know about great-uncle Eric who died in a Liverpool hotel after consuming too many oysters after backing the winner of the Grand National, if Granny hadn't told me?

My Wise Granny was also the guardian of lotions and potions. She had a secret store of gripe water, syrup of figs and other traditional remedies for childish ailments and could always find a dock leaf to rub on a nettle sting. Her extensive repertoire of superstitions and old wives' tales included infallible methods of weather forecasting; she taught us to scan the clouds for enough blue sky to make a pair of sailor's trousers, and to look in the fields to see if the cows were lying down (a sure sign it was going to rain). She also used to issue rather alarming warnings – her favourite being, 'If you don't stop making that face, my dear, the wind will change and it will be stuck forever.' 'Like Aunt Ethel's?' we would reply.

Yoga Granny

A long, drawn-out 'Om', regularly repeated, comes from Granny's bedroom. She's wearing her really cool yoga pants and sharing her mat with two grand-children, having coaxed their flexible young limbs into the Lotus position. Together they have mastered the Downward Dog pose, the Cat and the Warrior (*so* enabling).

Granny has difficulty with the Camel, and falls over when she tries to stand on her head. But since she exchanged instant coffee for Instant Karma (courtesy of John Lennon, 1971 – Granny's heyday), she's definitely calmer. She goes round smiling enigmatically and singing under her breath, 'Well we all shine on, Like the moon and the stars and the sun.'

Praise for Jane Fearnley-Whittingstall's
The Good Granny Guide

"Granny Jane gets the golden rules right.
She is absolutely spot on." *The Times*

"Gives tips on how to spoil the grandkids without
ruining your relationship with their
Mum and Dad." *Woman's Own*

"Even perfect grandmas could pick up a trick or
two from this witty compilation of
first-hand advice." *Mail on Sunday*

In case of difficulty in purchasing any Short Books
title through normal channels, please contact
BOOKPOST Tel: 01624 836000
Fax: 01624 837033
email: bookshop@enterprise.net
www.bookpost.co.uk
Please quote ref. 'Short Books'